Investing

Techniques For Constructing An Lucrative Assortment Of
Investment Properties Accompanied By In-depth Market
Analysis

*(Methods For Constructing A Lucrative Investment
Portfolio Via Real Estate)*

Eleazar Vazquez

TABLE OF CONTENT

Collaborate with a seasoned Real Estate Expert

One can independently locate a residence... but what is the rationale? The merchant covers the specialist fees, which include the expenses of the buyer's representative, hence it is advisable to take advantage of this opportunity. I have previously acquired properties that were listed as "for sale by owner" (FSBO) at favorable prices, although this is not universally applicable. There is an abundance of For Sale By Owner (FSBO) properties that are excessively priced.

The vendors are abstaining from employing an agent due to the fact that their owed amount exceeds the property's value. They may endeavor to convince you that the property offers favorable terms, yet exercise caution. If, perchance, you are able to discern a property being assessed directly as a FSBO, and subsequently convince the vendor to divulge the remuneration they would typically incur by engaging an agent, it may prove to be a favorable transaction for you. However, frequently the optimal approach to acquaint oneself with advantageous transactions is to collaborate with a highly-networked real estate broker.

One of the benefits of collaborating with a representative is their ability to provide you with equivalent deals in close proximity, as well as their extensive network that ensures a smooth and seamless process for the research and financing. A decent dealer will deal with pretty much every part of the home buy for you.

Another significant advantage of utilizing a broker is their immediate access to properties not yet on the market. The individual will be inclined to promptly contact you via telephone or email should the property meet your preferences. If you are embarking on this endeavor independently, it is possible that you may lack any prior acquaintance with the property until you inadvertently encounter it during your search, potentially subjecting it to alternate propositions by that time.

Does Your Primary Residence Constitute an Investment?

Numerous individuals ponder the adequacy of their primary residence as a viable investment.

The optimal reply would be, "Indeed, that is partly true and partly false."

It is widely acknowledged that land prices typically experience annual increments. With an annualized growth rate of 6%, the value of the house you acquire at present is projected to double within approximately twelve years, and quadruple within approximately 24 years. At that point, it is plausible that you would have fully discharged the payment, thus suggesting a prudent endeavor. Your residence contributes to your overall net worth, although unlike investment properties that appreciate your net worth and generate consistent income, it incurs ongoing expenses. Evidently, there exists a discernible disparity between endeavors that generate profits and those that entail financial losses.

The primary manner in which your own residence will ever generate income is when it is sold. Please bear this in mind when determining the extent of your financial capacity for a home. If, by chance, you are able to locate a sufficiently pleasant location and incur lesser expenses, it would be more sensible to pursue such an option and allocate the surplus funds towards an investment property.

Nonetheless, as a collective entity, we generate income for the purpose of its expenditure and the improvement of our quality of life. Due to this rationale, we actively contribute... in order to maintain an enhanced quality of life. If owning a sizable residence is of utmost importance to you and within your financial means, why not consider it? Do not regard it with the same mindset as you would towards your speculative assets.

Derive inspiration from the principles exemplified by Warren Buffett. The individual known as the "Prophet of Omaha" is widely regarded as the preeminent stock market and business investor in history, with an estimated net worth of $82.3 billion. Nonetheless, his primary place of residence, even at the ripe age of 90, remains a comparable dwelling he acquired back in 1958 for a sum of $31,500, which presently translates to approximately $250,000. It is currently valued at an anticipated amount of $652,619. He regards it as the third most successful investment he has ever made. Possessing a large and lavish dwelling holds no inherent importance for him. He has had the opportunity to both accumulate and divest himself of wealth.

Do not resign from your current occupation prematurely.

Similar to most individuals, I am aware that you are likely eager to resign from your current employment. Everyone desires the day when they will achieve financial independence. Despite the irrefutable evidence that investing in real estate offers a rapid path to wealth, it should be noted that it is far from being a get-rich-quick scheme. Taking all factors into account, there are numerous benefits for novice investors.

Engaging in land investment does not require a substantial time commitment, and it can be conveniently pursued during one's discretionary hours. Managing a property once it has been chosen and the transaction has been completed is quite straightforward, necessitating only a few hours per month for each property in most cases.

I would like to recommend that you personally attend to the limited number of assets you initially possess. This endeavor necessitates a certain level of financial commitment, which is crucial for two primary reasons. First and foremost, you will experience a shortfall in funds, and through self-sufficiency, you can accumulate savings. Furthermore, it will assist you in managing the aforementioned property related matters. In that manner, should your property manager ever relay a falsehood to you, you will possess the knowledge and discernment to recognize it.

Once you are ready to engage the services of a property manager, it is imperative to carefully select the right candidate. In the event that you happen to engage the services of a competent property manager, you will promptly appreciate that the cost involved is not significantly higher than self-managing the property (unless, of course, you also perform the maintenance tasks yourself). A standard supervisory group imposes fees ranging between 5% and 10%, depending on factors such as the property's age, location, and size. The supervisory committee typically provides assistance to individual staff members, and offers more cost-effective solutions for resolving a particular issue compared to an independently contracted worker.

Furthermore, skilled (please note that I emphasize "skilled" and not "small, family-owned") organizations will carry out preventive maintenance tasks that you may procrastinate on, thus resulting in even greater savings in the long run.

Once you have attained a level of income commensurate with that of your primary employment, you will then have the option to discontinue your current occupation, if desired. However, it is important to bear in mind that prematurely ceasing your endeavors may result in financial strain, leading to the adoption of short-sighted business strategies influenced by immediate mortgage obligations rather than taking into account the overall investment value in the long run. Moreover, retaining your profession also enhances the ease with which you can acquire real estate. It is easier to convince a financial institution (or dealer) that you will be capable of meeting your payments if you can demonstrate that the funds used to purchase the property are merely additional income, while your primary employment effectively covers your usual expenses.

Error: Holding the Anticipation of Receiving Comprehensive Guidance

In the first place, individuals who possess a genuine understanding of their responsibilities typically lack the necessary amount of time to dedicate entirely to your needs or provide comprehensive instructions on every aspect. Furthermore, it is impolite to make such inquiries. However, it is crucial to note that this approach is not conducive to achieving the highest level of success.

You possess a unique identity. Your success will derive from something uniquely your own. It is unlikely that what proved effective for someone else will yield similar results for you. The rationale behind your involvement in the realm of business and contribution may be shared by others who came before you, but your unique approach towards accomplishing your objectives should be tailored to align with your personal values and interests. Striving to replicate someone else's actions closely resembles asserting that one must adopt a specific persona to achieve success. It is highly impractical to engage in such an endeavor. Furthermore, what would be the underlying justification for your intention? Each individual's path to success will vary, and no two individuals will follow an identical route.

However, you have the ability to incorporate ideas and principles from diverse origins while expressing your own unique style. Please refrain from perceiving this as a call to excessively complicate your process by scattering various fragments throughout and laboriously organizing them. However, it is crucial to recognize that success is achieved when you acquire diverse components gradually, and subsequently integrate them into a cohesive system tailored to your needs.

If one diligently seeks guidance, whether through personal interaction or the study of authoritative texts, one can effectively strive to replicate their methodologies. However, remain receptive throughout the journey to acquiring supplementary resources that may pertain to your distinct individual achievements.

Error: Placing Faith in Others' Assertions

It is imperative to exercise caution not only in the information you consume and the sources from which you seek guidance, but also to refrain from unquestioningly accepting everything presented to you as a real estate investor, as it could lead to a tumultuous journey. There will be numerous individuals endeavoring to offer advice regarding what actions you ought to take and avoid.

(despite lacking knowledge of the appropriate actions), yet significantly, there will invariably be a vendor attempting to persuade you as to the merits of acquiring a specific investment property. Provided that you seek to gain further guidance and cultivate the capacity to ultimately make independent decisions, uninfluenced by others' opinions, your insights will be as commendable as they come.

There appears to be a disparity in the level of trust within this particular segment, which differs from the trust previously discussed in the segment entitled You Will Have to Trust Other People. There exists a multitude of types of relationships within any given industry. The preceding dialogue pertains to the importance of placing trust in others in order to avail oneself of opportunities during one's journey. In order to avoid shouldering all responsibilities oneself, it becomes necessary to enlist others to take charge of specific tasks. This is the juncture in which it becomes imperative to ascertain the means to place trust in others, while maintaining due diligence in verification.

The trust I refer to in this passage pertains not to entrusting someone with specific tasks on your behalf, but rather to earnestly considering the words and statements of others. If you rely solely on someone's account of an agreement, it indicates that you have not conducted the necessary research and investigation on your own. Furthermore, if you fail to conduct thorough and comprehensive research on properties prior to their acquisition, you are exposing yourself to the risk of jeopardizing your investment career, as if a meteor were to strike.

Be aware that there is scarcely anything regarding a land transaction that you cannot verify.

For instance, when acquiring an investment property, it is advisable to thoroughly scrutinize all of the estimated figures to the best of your ability. Determine the aggregate local charge through the utilization of the expenditure evaluator's website, obtain an authentic insurance quotation, and consult multiple property managers or real estate agents specialized in rentals to obtain their estimation on the potential rental income for the specific property in question. Actuals for fixes and opening are unavailable. If you are engaged in the process of property flipping or rehabilitating, it is advisable to conduct a comprehensive property inspection and obtain multiple cost estimates for the necessary work (including a potential 10% contingency allowance for potential budgetary overruns during the rehabilitation process). Subsequently, you may engage in a thorough investigation concerning matters such as the property's title and other factors that have the potential to give rise to issues. There are various methods available to ascertain practically every aspect concerning a property. The only

Factors that cannot be ascertained or controlled with certainty are unpredictable variables that may lead to unforeseen circumstances beyond anticipatory knowledge.

Throughout the entire process of conducting due diligence, it was not necessary for you to place trust in the words of others. Instead, you independently verified and examined every aspect. It is imperative that you demonstrate self-reliance in actively participating in the investigative aspect. Indeed, while you may leverage others as valuable resources and extract information from them, ultimately, the determination to proceed with a project or withdraw should be made solely by you, based on your individual verification procedures.

The most effective approach to reach a point where one can conduct thorough and comprehensive due diligence is through proper education and training. Education is the mechanism through which one can refrain from relying on the information provided by others and instead acquire the ability to independently comprehend the nature of their pursuits.

Therefore, it is essential to bear in mind that it is necessary to have confidence in others and delegate everyday tasks to them. However, when it comes to your investment decisions, it is crucial that they are solely made by you, relying on your own knowledge and expertise to make informed choices.

The author does not possess professional qualifications in law or accounting, and therefore, the information presented in this section of the book should not be construed as legal or accounting advice. We would highly recommend consulting your legal and accounting counsel before proceeding with the execution of any tax or legal tactics pertaining to your investment activities on Airbnb.

Establishing a limited liability company is completely discretionary. If you are commencing a small-scale venture, it may not be imperative for you to initiate the establishment of your Limited Liability Company (LLC). It is understandable that certain individuals may choose to conserve their financial resources for potential future expenses.

Eventually, once you begin generating income from your Airbnb business, it is likely that you will establish it.

What is an LLC?

An LLC, known as a Limited Liability Company, encompasses a business framework that offers safeguarding for your enterprise while serving as a means to leverage tax advantages and liability benefits for business proprietors. There are numerous advantages associated with the establishment of a Limited Liability Company (LLC).

Asset Protection: This entails that in the event a guest accommodated in your Airbnb sustains an injury or experiences a fall and subsequently attempts to initiate a legal claim against you, it will not be feasible due to your ownership of a Limited Liability Company. You, as an individual, are immune from personal liability in this matter; instead, legal action will be directed towards the business entity. It is crucial to consider that the entire operation of Airbnb is safeguarded by a Limited Liability Company (LLC), including all assets and aspects encompassed within the enterprise. The individual endeavoring to file a lawsuit against you will solely have recourse to the assets contained within your business for litigation purposes. They are legally prohibited from pursuing any of your assets, such as automobiles, additional ventures, and so forth, as the incident took place within the confines of the company.

Therefore, the limited liability company serves as a safeguard against legal actions and any financial obligations as well. In the event of the business's bankruptcy, it shall have no impact on you. Additionally, it should be noted that in the event of any loans associated with the business, there is no cause for concern as they will not be linked to your personal identity.

Tax Advantages: An LLC offers numerous favorable tax incentives. For instance, all the items you have purchased for your business can be deducted, thus exempting you from taxation on these expenses. Should you desire further information regarding the tax advantages of an LLC, it is encouraged that you engage in a conversation with either a tax advisor or legal counsel.

You can establish a corporate account utilizing the Employer Identification Number (EIN) obtained in conjunction with your Limited Liability Company (LLC) registration, allowing you to pursue business financing options. Acquiring an EIN number upon starting an LLC can yield significant advantages. An Employer Identification Number (EIN) serves a similar function as a social security number does for individuals, but specifically for your business. It constitutes an autonomous entity of its own, affording you the opportunity to establish a business account and secure loans for said business. Consequently, establishing an LLC effectively enhances the perceived legitimacy of your business. It is not comparable to a sole proprietorship or any similar entity. On the contrary, having an LLC establishes your legal legitimacy.

An additional inquiry that holds value is, "Is it advantageous to obtain an LLC for one's business?" To which the response would be affirmative. If you intend to engage in long-term Airbnb hosting, it would be advisable to establish a limited liability company (LLC).

Methods to Obtain a Limited Liability Company (LLC)

There exist multiple avenues through which one can establish an LLC, however, I would strongly advocate for procuring your certification through the reputable service provider, LegalZoom. It is a straightforward process in which all you need to do is visit legalzoom.com and conduct a search for the desired name that you wish to utilize for your LLC or business. Subsequently, select the state; subsequently, respond to the subsequent inquiries. If you do not possess the requisite knowledge pertaining to LLCs, we recommend referring to the platform legalzoom.com. Additionally, you can contact them via telephone, where they will likely provide you with instructions or guidance. It is genuinely one of the simplest tasks.

Is it appropriate for me to don virtual reality goggles?

Indeed, interactive training sessions and meetings are among the myriad of activities within the metaverse that extensively rely on virtual reality equipment. Therefore, companies such as magic Leap and Varjo, known for producing virtual reality spectacles, as well as Gleechi and Ultraleap, which specialize in hand monitoring and virtual elements manipulation, are certainly deserving of attention.

Warping entered into a collaboration with H&M, an additional technology company, in order to offer their clientele immersive virtual reality experiences within the physical store setting.

Nevertheless, there is a limited proportion of children who engage in Minecraft or Roblox while utilizing virtual reality goggles. They are predominantly engaged in smartphone usage.

Prior to donning spectacles, we shall employ our mobile devices to engage in augmented reality experiences, such as virtually trying on garments prior to making a purchase or conducting cosmetic tests.

What were the primary hazards associated with the Metaverse?

Legal professionals caution that there will be an abundance of disputes arising from diverse matters such as ownership disputes, intellectual property conflicts, content licensing issues, data protection concerns, and risks linked to cryptocurrency assets within the Metaverse. Multiple legal proceedings will be required to establish the guidelines; for example, in September 2021, Roblox reached a resolution with the US National Music Publishers Association, granting musicians the opportunity to debut their songs within the Metaverse.

The primary concern for investors lies in ascertaining whether companies possess a genuine comprehension of the intricacies involved in crafting an enthralling metaverse that users would not only be inclined to participate in, but also be compelled to return to.

Certain entrepreneurs may face challenges if they opt for the "build it and they will come" approach. The ultimate result will be expeditiously ascertained. The most exceptional teams will emerge victorious.

An additional matter of concern is the possibility of the virtual realm remaining excessively fragmented, thereby hindering users from seamlessly migrating their digital identities across various platforms.

Numerous companies are currently vying to become the prevailing means of connecting disparate digital ecosystems. However, a significant concern lies in the absence of a distinct frontrunner, as this could ultimately lead to fragmented factions.

Is there a possibility that major technology titans like Microsoft and Facebook will dominate the Metaverse, and if so, would this have a significant impact?

A dispute is emerging regarding the potential dominance of a singular corporation, such as Google, versus a consortium of companies collaborating collectively.

In the realm of virtual reality, Zuckerberg's provision entails a significant degree of centralized authority over an entire ecosystem. Conversely, in the domain of blockchain technology, we observe a diverse array of virtual currencies coexisting and numerous enterprises engaging, serving as a prime demonstration of an alternative paradigm. It is our belief that this conflict will persist for a decade to come.

The Sandbox, an online gaming platform centered around cryptocurrencies, epitomizes the notion of a decentralized virtual universe.

A significant number of observers of the metaverse question Facebook's capacity to govern the Metaverse. Many metaverse analysts doubt Facebook's capability to establish dominion over the Metaverse.

Numerous developers in the metaverse exhibit a shared goal of promoting transparency and decentralization. However, the realization of this vision necessitates the presence of a diverse range of participants and healthy competition. If these prominent entities fail to effectively navigate the intricacies of delivering virtual worlds and related experiences, it is doubtful that they will prevail.

As previously exemplified by Twitch, the leading contender in the realm of the Metaverse will inevitably emerge through competition with their counterparts.

It is indeed fascinating to observe the inclusion of Microsoft or Facebook in the Metaverse, as this presents significant opportunities for growth and expansion. Nevertheless, given the previous demonstration by Twitch, it is evident that the dominant entity within the Metaverse will emerge as a competitive force within the industry.

Can it be concluded that the current hype surrounding the Metaverse is unwarranted?

Not at all. While extensive coverage on the Metaverse and its potential to revolutionize the future currently exists, there remains a dearth of information regarding investment opportunities in this domain. In April 2021, Epic Games successfully concluded a fundraising round of $1 billion, led by Sony Corporation, whereas The Sandbox, an alternative gaming platform, secured a Series B investment round of $93 million with the significant support of SoftBank. In actuality, these substantial funding agreements remain exceptions.

Web 3.0 and investments in cryptocurrencies prevail as prominent subjects in financial news, with a strong focus on monetary value. However, this holds significant importance as the industry is still in its nascent stage, constantly evolving with daily advancements in various applications. It should be noted that the associated figures are seldom extraordinarily high.

Tailwind, a prominent game company, aspires to position itself among the enterprises set to receive substantial funding in the upcoming fiscal year.

Overall, financiers are currently in a state of anticipation as they assess the potential value of emerging enterprises before making any investment decisions. The majority of financing rounds have been attributed to Series A and Seed investment sessions.

The upcoming year holds significant importance. Prominent investment firms such as Coatue and Sequoia are closely monitoring these initiatives and have alluded to substantial capital allocations. They are carefully observing the startup ventures that have successfully secured seed funding and are prepared to invest in three to four select enterprises.

It will truly flourish when we are able to engage in genuine collaborative creation.

It is likely that we still require a couple of years before reaching the point where we can seamlessly transition between applications. Nonetheless, we are of the opinion that its true potential will be unleashed when we have the opportunity to collaborate and engage with individuals from various geographical locations, all while diligently undertaking diverse pursuits."

Host Amenities in Airbnb

The majority of novice individuals frequently inquire about the amenities to include in their listings. What are the particular aspects that guests tend to value the most? Which items are to be excluded? In this particular segment, we shall proceed with enumerating the top ten amenities, starting from the tenth position and concluding at the first. Here are a few closely guarded hosting strategies, along with all the valuable insights I have gained from hosting more than 3,000 guests.

The following recommendations, strategies, and exemplary methods are centered around assisting novice hosts in maximizing their earnings, attracting exceptional guests, and expediting the attainment of super host status. If you are unfamiliar with hosting on Airbnb, this would be suitable for you.

As a proprietor of Airbnb, it is essential to be aware that guests frequently opt for a stay at an Airbnb rather than a hotel, seeking a distinctive and memorable experience. That experience may manifest in different ways, such as the provision of a kitchen, additional living space, a sofa, or even a private entrance. Regardless of the underlying cause, as a host, it is essential to impress your guests in order to attain that highly sought-after five-star review. This principle holds true regardless of the valuation of your property, whether it is a luxurious $1000 per night accommodation or a more modest $50 per night lodging; the significance remains unchanged. The objective is to surpass the expectations of your guests, especially considering that the majority of us do not engage in hosting at the thousand dollars a night level.

Let us examine the prevailing amenities that are essential to include in your Airbnb listing. In the event that you accommodate guests in the upscale price range of one thousand dollars per night, it is imperative to have at least one of the following 10 items. Let us commence

Welcome Binder

In the welcome compendium, it is imperative to incorporate a formal letter of welcome, a concise enumeration of household regulations, and a comprehensive manual with identical content to that presented in your Airbnb listing. Furthermore, please ensure that the binder contains local suggestions, as well as exclusive local offers and vouchers.

Cleaning Supplies

If you wish for your guests to take responsibility for cleaning up after themselves, it is imperative to ensure the availability of cleaning supplies. Currently, visitors exhibit heightened concerns regarding sanitization and the transmission of microorganisms, thus making hand sanitizers and disinfecting wipes indispensable.

Toiletries

Guests forget things often. Given that you are operating an Airbnb rather than a hotel, it is not feasible for guests to access toothpaste while comfortably dressed in their sleeping attire during the late hours. Anticipate any possible oversights on behalf of your guests and ensure that those items are readily available to them.

Mobile Device Chargers" or "Chargers for Cellular Phones

Forgetting one's cell phone charger while on a trip is an especially unfavorable circumstance. Ensure appropriate inventory of the frequently utilized options specific to your geographic area, and typically spanning global markets. That will serve as a charger compatible with the iPhone, specifically designed for fast charging capabilities. For Android smartphones, it is recommended to procure a USB cable compatible with either the USB, Micro B, or USB C interface. Conduct a few searches on the Amazon platform to locate phone chargers, where you may also come across a charger designed with multiple ends to accommodate various phone models.

Snacks and Drinks

Frequently, visitors arrive with an appetite and a need for refreshment. Although I am not proposing that you offer artisanal bread or organic fruit harvested from your own garden, it is advisable to at least supply a selection of dry goods such as granola, energy bars, potato chips, nuts, and other non-perishable items in the refrigerator. Please ensure that there is chilled water available, along with optional beverages such as soda or carbonated drinks. First and foremost, ensure that you have coffee and tea readily accessible. There is nothing more distressing than awakening in the morning and realizing that one is devoid of coffee. This particular item holds significant prominence within my reviews, and its returns exceed expectations due to its minimal stocking costs.

Varieties of Pillows" "Various Categories of Pillows" "Diverse Assortment of Pillows" "Assorted Pillow Types" "Various Classifications of Pillows

In each of my accommodations, I consistently ensure that there are four pillows placed on the bed. Two of the pillows possess a firmer composition, while the remaining two exhibit a softer constitution. Astonishing as it may seem, the selection of an inappropriate pillow has the capacity to entirely dictate one's perception of comfort when it comes to a bed. If you harbor any skepticism, I would encourage you to conduct an experiment within the confines of your bed. Simply opt for a pillow of a variant nature than your customary choice, and subsequently evaluate its performance throughout the night. I surmise that your previously agreeable sleeping accommodations may become less accommodating, leading to a night of restlessness.

Parking

If there is a lack of availability of a parking space associated with your listing, ensure that comprehensive documentation of nearby parking alternatives is provided, complete with estimated costs for each option. Make this information readily accessible and prepared for your esteemed guests.

A hairdryer, as well as an iron and ironing board" or "An assortment of amenities including a hairdryer, iron, and ironing board

I am unable to express the frequency with which I have previously responded to this question prior to a guest's arrival. Therefore, it is advised to ensure that your unit is equipped with essential appliances, such as a hairdryer, an ironing board, and an iron, based on my recommendation.

Workspace

It is probable that there will be a decrease in corporate travel whilst there is anticipated growth in recreational travel. A significant portion of the travel for leisure purposes will involve remote workers conducting their work from the comfort of your residence. Ensure that you possess a suitable workspace consisting of a desk, a ergonomic chair, and at least a multifunctional area, such as a kitchen table or an adjustable laptop table that can be positioned over a sofa.

CHAPTER 6

Cash

It represents a more secure investment opportunity due to its heightened level of safety, although its rate of return is relatively low.

It generally pertains to the current timeframe, typically spanning a period of fewer than 90 days, and yields a financial return in the form of revenue disbursements.

Some of the most lucrative financial investments include certificates of deposit, government treasury funds, short-term corporate funds, S&P 500 index funds, dividend equity funds, and municipal bond funds.

"Various forms of monetary investments:

• Savings account. The fee charged for borrowing these documents is of negligible amount.

• Money market. Collective investment schemes that allocate your funds into cash or cash equivalents with very short-term maturity, typically less than six months. The longer the store remains open, the higher the financing expenses will be. You are more likely to obtain a larger premium on those as opposed to excessively high premium bank accounts. The premium you acquire remains constant and does not fluctuate, allowing you to select the desired duration for your investment. One drawback is the lack of access to your funds during the designated period. You will indeed need to withdraw beforehand; however, there will be a cost incurred, comprising both an interest rate and a fee. An additional adverse perspective to consider pertains to the agreed upon interest rate. In the event that the loan cost increases within the agreed duration, your term deposit will not be considered as yours, given that it was initially secured under favorable interest conditions.

• Certificate of deposit (CD). You agree to maintain a lump sum deposit in pristine condition for a specified duration, and as a result, the bank will grant you an interest rate incentive. They are alternatively referred to as CDs. If you choose to withdraw prematurely, there will be penalties which may vary depending on the financial institution. To safeguard your funds, please refrain from making any premature withdrawals to avoid financial loss.

• Capital held in fixed-term accounts. Providing a predetermined interest rate for a specified duration in exchange for safekeeping.

• Cash Isas. Money or offers Isa. The foremost benefit of an Individual Savings Account (ISA) lies in the opportunity to generate returns on your savings, all while exempting them from taxation (up to a specific threshold, currently set at £20,000 in the United Kingdom). You have the option to annually add to the amount, however, you are limited to opening only one Cash ISA per year. However, it is feasible to initiate a transfer of funds from one Cash Isa to another with a different provider. The allocation for the Isa encompasses both cash and shares Isa, thereby allowing for the division of the £20,000 limit between these respective investments. Certain suppliers provide a flexible individual savings account (ISA) option, enabling the withdrawal and replacement of funds within the same tax year. Kindly inquire with your supplier regarding the availability of this service.

The Individual Savings Account (ISA) in Britain serves as the British equivalent of the IRA, which is commonly recognized in the United States.

"The advantages of a financial investment:

" • When allocating funds to a bank account, assurance is provided for their security.

• You can rest assured that funds will be available in the future.

The drawbacks/demerits/disadvantages of monetary investments:

• Low returns

• Account charges. On occasion, these expenditures may surpass the designated limit.

The financial burden imposed upon you and the detrimental impact on your investment

You have the option to establish a financial speculation account through online platforms, over the phone, or at a nearby banking institution.

4. Exercise caution when approached by an individual of unclad nature who presents to you the opportunity to acquire a garment from his own possession.

Jill and Linda had been closest companions since their time in school, and their shared aspiration of establishing their own business had materialized successfully. Located in a diverse neighborhood, stood the Eyeliner Diner, emanating an atmosphere of vibrant liveliness. In a short span of a few years, they had also witnessed a substantial growth of the region surrounding their business. The previously hazardous locality has now transformed into a trendy area where young professionals engage in bidding wars to purchase properties. Jill and Linda required participation in the ongoing surge in land demand in close proximity.

Their plan entailed acquiring properties, refurbishing them with the interests of this young professional buyer in mind, and possibly even locating potential buyers by distributing flyers at their café (instead of engaging a real estate agent), with the objective of reaping substantial profits from selling at a significantly higher price than the purchase and renovation costs.

Jill was irresistibly drawn to the chance to observe a discourse led by an expert who had secured a seat at table #16, where the topic of discussion was the practice colloquially referred to as "flipping houses." It was the exact content that she sincerely desired to listen to. They engaged in conversation with a highly reliable individual named Rick, and Jill and Linda thought they had witnessed the formation of an ideal partnership.

Rick would take it upon himself to locate the arrangements and subsequently reconfigure them. Their only requirement was to procure the necessary funds and provide guidance regarding the appropriate approach to captivate the enthusiastic demographic of young professionals who eagerly embraced any product or service introduced to the local market. The majority of their time was consumed by the operations at the Eyeliner Diner, making Rick the ideal candidate for Jill and Linda due to his role as both a scout and contractor.

Subsequently, Rick presented the budding financiers with a proposition that appeared to offer significant latitude, half a month later. Rick advised that they obtain a comprehensive assessment, encompassing both the current market value and the projected post-repair value, to gain a more thorough understanding of their potential profit margins. Whom would it be advisable for them to enlist in order to assess the property? Rick was acquainted with an individual who possessed the capability to handle that matter on their behalf. Moreover, such was the case with Rick. He possessed a solution for every inquiry, even pertaining to the whereabouts of the funds required for the acquisition of the property. Rick connected them with a financially secure institution capable of providing funds for 65% of the purchase price as well as the renovations.

Jill and Linda eagerly anticipated witnessing the realization of their plans, just like the Eyeliner Diner. They made a significant financial investment and now Rick was prepared to commence the renovation of their inaugural property in unison. However, prior to his completion of the first transaction, he stumbled upon yet another exceptional opportunity. The second deal was executed with even greater efficiency, owing to their prior experience. Moreover, confidence was collaborating with Rick as he attended to every minute detail, while Jill and Linda concentrated their efforts on the success of their restaurant.

The completion of the initial arrangement's remodeling experienced several delays, and astonishingly enough, Rick came across a third arrangement that Jill and Linda were eager to seize promptly, lest they forego the opportunity. Exhausted of their financial reserves, they earnestly anticipated resorting to one of the two remaining options in order to obtain funds for purchasing the third item. Rick concocted another arrangement. Revising the initial agreement to transform it into a conventional residential mortgage and settling the exorbitant interest cash loan. Rick had recently acquired the individual's assistance in that matter as well. At that time, the bank had the discretion to select the appraiser, and thus the same appraiser who had previously assessed the properties was also tasked with conducting the revaluation for negotiations.

Jill and Linda were elated by the substantial outcome of the examination, considering the complete repayment of the loan and all the renovation expenses, as well as the retrieval of their entire down payment along with a surplus sum. With an abundant sum of money obtained from the renegotiation, they proceeded to acquire the third arrangement. Given the satisfactory performance of the equation, they ultimately proceeded to re-negotiate the second and third sales agreements as well.

A discrepancy arose at the initiation of the fourth arrangement with respect to the course of events. Why did the initial strategy fail to generate sales? They had assumed that nearby residences were flying off the market, yet their property remained unsold for a period exceeding 120 days? Similarly, Rick had become increasingly difficult to capture when they contacted him. There was typically an alternative justification for his actions. Moreover, his presence at the Diner was diminishing as well.

With the utilization of three conventional home loans in the initial three arrangements and one hard cash advance in the fourth arrangement, the monthly payments began to significantly deplete their financial resources. They were on the verge of feeling cold when a proposal was presented regarding deal #1. However, their initial enthusiasm dissipated rapidly upon witnessing

It is evident that the proposition sum was considerably lower than the cost estimate. To be honest, the amount owed was not as substantial. Perplexed, they inquired the specialist who had documented the property, a."

The means by which Rick's contact was possible, how was such a concept feasible? He attributed it solely to an undervalued proposal and advised against fixating on it. Nevertheless, at that juncture, the specialist continued to offer nearly identical incentives to bolster their sales efforts. In the end, it turned out that the specialist recommended by Rick was a recent entrant in the industry and was equally surprised, just like Jill and Linda, when the same transactions revealed a value significantly lower than what the revaluation had indicated.

During this period, Rick was indeed difficult to contact and currently finding himself without any support, they made the decision to accept the offer and intend to see it through to the conclusion while carrying cash. They were further astounded to discover an extensive catalogue of concerns during the examination. The investigator discovered an unforeseen truth that differed from what Jill and Linda were aware of. It seems that the quality of the workmanship was extremely poor, with shortcuts taken at every opportunity and occasional failures to meet code requirements during the repairs. Prior to engaging in a discussion with Rick regarding the examination, the purchaser withdrew their support.

At this juncture, it can be asserted that Rick was absolutely unable to acquire his telephone in any capacity. The duo commenced reaching out to the acquaintances they had encountered via Rick in an effort to establish an alternative means of communication with him, yet each individual expressed a synchronous challenge in being able to apprehend him formerly. Rick had essentially vanished. Furthermore, meanwhile, they were promptly beginning to lag behind in fulfilling their contractual obligations.

Jill and Linda witnessed the manifestation of their aspirations for home flipping turn into an unfortunate nightmare. They conferred with a number of discreet organizations in an endeavor to ascertain whether their unfortunate circumstances entailed fraud or any activities that might be deemed illegal, as they suspected they were the targets of a heinous conspiracy. Regrettably, regardless of the dire situation they found themselves in, it proved challenging to ascertain any genuine misconduct. The assessments, while remarkably elevated, remained within the parameters dictated by the examination guidelines. Indeed, the reports were unquestionably based on the most superior data, though there was nothing that could be deemed misleading or untruthful. The difficult cash lender had relied upon the current condition assessments, yet in three out of the four transactions, he had been proven incorrect.

Addressed and upon the fourth instance, his 65% credit to esteem ratio remained satisfactory for him in the event of default. The contractual renegotiation agent incurred substantial initial expenses, although nothing remarkably unusual in its entirety. Although Rick was subject to scrutiny from a supervisor due to his consistently subpar performance and exorbitant charges for his contracting services, it should be noted that he did not engage in any unlawful activities.

After extensive analysis, they arrived at an evident inference and comprehended that Rick had garnered substantial profits from them. He wholesaled every arrangement he found to them, amassing significant upfront profits. Subsequently, he significantly amplified his earnings in his capacity as a contractor by excessively inflating his charges. After considering all pertinent factors, it was concluded that within a span of approximately six months, he had accrued an estimated total of $150,000 from them. After the complete depletion of their monetary resources and assets, he departed and moved on to his next target.

Jill and Linda ultimately pursued financial security, resulting in the unfortunate loss of all their purchased properties and the entirety of their invested funds. Additionally, they were compelled to divest their successful Eyeliner Diner enterprise. They comprehended an exceptionally complex assemblage of illustrations concerning real estate. Despite expending their entire resources, they discovered remarkable instances of land investment.

Envisioning the Landscape of the Future through the

Time is running. What existed in the past will not be present in the future. Rapid transformations are occurring at a significant pace. With the advent of advanced and sophisticated technology, certain occupations are inevitably poised to become obsolete. There is a forthcoming decline in several conventional industries.

Items once considered highly valued have become obsolete. The aforementioned possessions, including VCRs, audio tapes, video tapes, and print photographs, are now devoid of any contemporary worth. The telegram is dead. There is a significant lack of individuals who engage in the act of sending postcards or inland letters.

In 1987, I acquired a laser printer at a cost of 1, 40,000, which is now obtainable at a mere one twentieth of its original price. The aforementioned statement holds true in regards to both computers and mobile phones.

I acquired three Ericsson mobile devices in the year 1995, each costing a sum of 36,000, during the commencement of mobile services in India. The aforementioned mobile device is now available for a reduced price of 1000 rupees, offering significantly enhanced features. Considering the significant decrease in call rates over the span of 15 years, it would be prudent to adopt a more impartial perspective when contemplating the future. During the World Economic Forum in Davos in 2016, it was asserted that the advent of the 4th Industrial Revolution is presently unfolding, inevitably resulting in the elimination of numerous employment opportunities due to rapid technological progress.

Alec Ross, in his book entitled 'The industries of the future', has provided a comprehensive analysis and rationale for how our future will unfold. Within his work, Ross discusses the anticipated advancements in industries and technology that will have far-reaching implications on various sectors, including businesses, service industries, and the general populace.

Indicators of the same phenomenon are arising if one observes with an unbiased perspective. Numerous sectors have experienced insolvency. Consider the case of Kodak, a brand that, not long ago, exclusively dealt in photo paper and enjoyed a monopoly. However, due to technological advancements and the passage of time, the company ultimately faced bankruptcy. Polaroid encountered a similar outcome to that of the company which was previously highly beloved by the financial industry. Xerox, situated in the league, was priced at US$ 60 in 2000 and is currently being traded at $7.

A similar outcome could potentially occur in the case of crude oil. In the foreseeable future, it is plausible that all forms of transportation could rely exclusively on electric battery technology, while prominent institutions may incorporate solar panels atop their buildings, potentially indicating the conclusion of the oil era. Petroleum will continue to remain unexplored beneath the surface of the earth. The coal industry will once again face significant setbacks. Germany has successfully transitioned over half of its energy requirements from conventional sources to renewable sources. Several other nations are following a similar trajectory.

The current issue we are confronting regarding the availability of drinking water will be effectively remedied through the process of desalinating seawater.

With the rise of mobile shopping, it is likely that the presence of local kirana shops, furniture stores, and various other retail establishments may gradually diminish, as individuals increasingly opt to place orders via mobile devices and have their purchases conveniently delivered to their homes.

A majority of small and medium enterprises are expected to face significant challenges. The majority of small and medium-sized share brokers are facing significant challenges in maintaining their business viability, as larger broking firms with ample resources have assumed control.

The utilization of technology will have an impact on every occupation. The agricultural sector is poised for a significant transformation as the costs of land, machinery, chemicals, and seeds are set to rise substantially. Advancements in technology will facilitate the implementation of economically efficient farming practices. The era of small-scale individual farmers is rapidly coming to a close. During an era of agricultural transformation, the control of farming practices is likely to shift from small-scale and economically disadvantaged farmers to affluent landowners and corporate entities. According to Alec Ross's analysis, it is projected that there will be agricultural robots priced at $100 in the foreseeable future. Farmers in developing nations will assume the role of field managers.

In the realm of labor, once more there will be profound transformations. It is evident that with the increasing automation of assembly lines, we are approaching a point where the majority, if not the entirety, of the production process will be carried out by robotic systems in the near future. In Japan, the ratio of robots to workers is 1500 per 10,000 individuals, with these robots exhibiting superior speed, quality, and cost-effectiveness. This phenomenon will gain momentum on a global scale. Similarly, news reporting will undergo transformation as automated software takes over the roles traditionally fulfilled by content writers, sub-editors, and news reporters.

As pertains to education, it is anticipated that there will be a proliferation of distance education courses and online coaching, thereby becoming more prevalent. Due to the alterations in systems, an individual of private status would be compelled to carefully deliberate numerous occasions prior to establishing expansive institutions and committing substantial financial resources. They, too, could potentially become obsolete due to advancements in technology.

Over the next 5-10 years, software is poised to bring significant disruption to a wide range of conventional industries. Consider the case of Uber or Ola. Presently, they have established themselves as the largest taxi service providers in the industry despite not possessing a single vehicle. Due to the implementation of sophisticated software, Air BNB has achieved the status of the largest hotel company, despite not possessing any physical hotel properties.

There will be modifications made to the judicial systems. Witnesses have the ability to submit their written testimonies and transmit them electronically to the courts. Numerous prominent legal entities have established their online platforms, providing individuals with the opportunity to seek guidance or procure legal document drafting services. And to what location shall these youthful legal practitioners find themselves directed? An additional peril posed to aspiring legal practitioners originates from the advent of legal software capable of assuming the various responsibilities currently undertaken by young lawyers, such as the exhaustive analysis of physical records to retrieve and synthesize pertinent information, as well as the drafting of trial-related documents.

The demand for accountants is set to decline once more, as small businesses increasingly adopt user-friendly software for their accounting needs, which are continually being introduced into the market. Automated self-service checkout systems will be implemented as a replacement for cashiers in banks and other establishments.

The IBM cognitive computing prototype, Watson, is poised to transform the field of medical diagnosis through its projected capacity to provide precise, reliable, and complimentary diagnoses of medical conditions. Physicians may potentially begin conducting virtual consultations, leveraging comprehensive electronic reports and online diagnostic capabilities, thereby alleviating the need for in-person visits. For significant surgeries and emergency situations, individuals may need to seek treatment at hospitals, or alternatively, hospitals may provide medical care at the patient's location.

If individuals have access to a majority of their essential needs within their households, it is likely that there will be a decrease in vehicular congestion on public thoroughfares, subsequently reducing the occurrences of traffic-related fatalities.

Automotive enterprises that have experienced significant growth in recent years may encounter a setback.

Due to the advancements in technology and the evolving nature of work systems, there exists a potential for a substantial decline in real estate values within major urban centers. Individuals may opt to relocate to more distant locations where the cost of land and housing units would be lower, as the absence of any further incentives to reside in major metropolitan areas may no longer prevail. The observed phenomenon in our nation, where individuals display a preference for residing in suburban areas, is likely evident to you. Property prices in Delhi have experienced a significant decline of approximately 30% over the past two to three years.

Human minds worldwide are engaged in the pursuit of enigmatic discoveries. We lack the knowledge or foresight regarding the dynamics of future developments. I do not wish to divert your attention from the primary idea that I have expounded upon thus far.

As informed investors, it is imperative for us to carefully evaluate all forthcoming developments prior to committing to any long-term investment in a particular stock.

Future is just future. It is possible to analyze and visualize it, and one can formulate speculations, but the exact outcome remains unknown.

Prior to concluding my investments and transitioning to trading, it would be remiss of me not to provide a comprehensive overview of the concept of investing in art and antiques.

Employing Your Purpose

Given the multitude of available strategies in real estate investment, it is imperative that you possess a clear understanding of your intended direction. Not only to maintain your persuasion along the way but also to aid you in determining the appropriate strategy for your needs. For example, upon the realization of the purpose behind my opportunities, I swiftly ascertain that wholesaling and flipping are not suitable strategies for me. Not only do both of those procedures entail a substantial amount of effort, but I have previously asserted that the type of work they entail is not work that I derive any form of enjoyment from. None of those aspects appear to be indicative of any potential for advancement or possibilities in my viewpoint. Upon reflection, it is evident why I opted for turnkey investment properties as my approach to real estate investing. The simplicity they offer aligns perfectly with my desire for autonomy, as these properties require significantly less involvement compared to traditional property ownership.

At this juncture, it is not necessary for you to possess an understanding of which systems align with your underlying rationale. At this juncture, it is crucial to comprehend the rationale behind your objectives so that as you progress further, you can ascertain whether or not different choices align with your underlying purpose. The purpose behind your endeavors may undergo modifications along the way, but the stronger your initial connection with it, the more effectively you can align your real estate investments with that objective.

The crucial aspect is to ensure that your underlying motivation remains at the forefront of your mind as you embark on the process of exploring various alternatives.

It is my earnest desire for you to acknowledge that I have indeed made a myriad of mistakes in the realm of real estate investment, and I am here to provide guidance in order to help you steer clear of those very same errors. I embarked upon my career in real estate investment as a publisher, subsequently accomplishing numerous property renovation and resale projects, acquiring both single and multi-family rental properties, developing undeveloped land, constructing new residential dwellings, and currently directing my attention primarily towards the acquisition of profitable vacation rental properties.

Since commencing my investments in Lifestyle Assets, I have experienced an unparalleled surge of vitality that surpasses any previous instances in my entire lifespan. The most promising opportunities for investing in profitable, income-generating rural estates lie ahead of us, rather than behind us. I am required to present the experience I have developed that delves into the acquisition, management, and promotion of a profitable vacation rental within the pages of this book.

This task is achievable by anyone, and it is highly recommended for individuals prioritizing the establishment of a sustainable lifestyle and financial independence. Constructing a profitable Lifestyle Asset portfolio does not entail an unduly intricate process, although it does necessitate acquiring knowledge about numerous variables, alongside the need to steer clear of prevalent misconceptions and errors. I am committed to discussing each and every one of them in detail within the pages of this book. There are a few important matters that you ought to be aware of right from the outset. 1) It is not possible to proceed with this transaction without providing any initial payment. You will have a stake in the matter. 2) It is advisable that you refrain from making arrangements to manage your personal assets. The final matter you require is an ensuing daily workload. 3) It is advisable for you to invest in properties that align with your own preferences and desires. The unique aspect of excursion rentals lies in their capacity for individual use, which sets them apart in a remarkable manner. 4) It is advisable for you to make a sustained contribution. Although there may be temporary benefits to owning Lifestyle Assets, they are ultimately long-term latent investments.

I am aware that there exists an element of incredulity. Whenever you direct your attention towards something, invest financial resources, or embark on a novel endeavor, a set of distinct inquiries will invariably arise within your mind. Allocating capital towards vacation rentals remains equivalent. However, I typically inform individuals that the principles we convey are grounded in rationality-based investing. As you commence the process of piecing together the fragments of the riddle, a comprehensive understanding of the master plan shall gradually unfold, lending an air of reassurance to your perception. You will successfully resolve the aforementioned issue, transitioning from contemplating the acquisition of a prosperous rural property to experiencing contentment in issuing a payment for your new Lifestyle Asset, as you have diligently attended to all necessary details and formalities.

Let us commence forthwith, address a subset of those inquiries, and proceed to discuss some of the strategies that we will employ in the future. This initial segment is associated with the organization of your promising future. One of the most significant errors I have made in the past was embarking on a new project without a clear vision of my destination.

In the year 2000, at a time when Teresa and I had recently completed our education and just entered into marital union, I embarked upon a professional opportunity which necessitated our relocation to Denver, Colorado. I had consistently possessed a strong interest in the field of real estate and began investing in my education. I devoted countless hours at Barnes and Noble, meticulously examining every book within my reach. Due to limited financial resources, my most favorable option was to acquire knowledge on the process of property refunds. I took a proactive approach and diligently located my initial property in the proximity of downtown Denver. The property I located demanded substantial effort but seemed to present a favorable opportunity for the given area. I distinctly remember feeling a profound sense of apprehension upon the mortgage holder's acceptance of my proposition. I was entirely unaware of the strategies you employed to secure the necessary funds for the transaction.

With my consent within reach, I promptly proceeded to attend the local real estate investment club gathering. I engaged in conversation with a few individuals who were potential listeners. One individual displayed a profound level of curiosity and subsequently made a formal request for me to remain present while he sought the presence of another individual. He reappeared shortly thereafter and introduced me to another gentleman of high regard who expressed his interest in procuring a property in this vicinity. Following a lapse of five minutes, he extended an offer to me.

Based on the assumption that I transfer my agreement to him, the amount would be $19,000. I was scarcely able to manage it. I had actively participated in the business and had recently engaged in the wholesale of my initial property. I proceeded directly to the bank in order to embark upon the process of cashing the check, and, as the adage goes, the subsequent events unfolded and became part of the past.

At that particular juncture, I was earning an annual income of $31,000. "I had recently achieved approximately 66%

concerning that amount during a singular weekend. I was thoroughly invigorated upon my return home, engaging in conversation with Teresa, and subsequently making the informed decision to relinquish my employment and embark upon my professional journey as a real estate investor. Teresa and I made the decision to relocate to Utah in order to embark on this new chapter in our lives.

We focused our efforts on acquiring properties that required renovation and intended to refurbish them before reselling, akin to the multi-property transformations depicted in contemporary television programs. I would diligently locate the properties and proceed to renovate them, while Teresa would actively contribute to strategizing and oversee their sale upon completion.

We successfully operated this business on a full-time basis for a duration of nearly six years. During that period, I typically portrayed myself as a real estate investor. On a certain occasion, I encountered an individual of higher social standing named George at a local association for land investors. He kindly informed me that I did not hold the status of an investor, but rather I was merely engaged in the occupation of renovating houses.

I will forever recollect this conversation considering the circumstance that my inner essence was suppressed. I had consistently been expressing with pride that, at the age of 23, I possessed the opportunity to depart from my current place of employment and embark on a career as a dedicated real estate investor. Currently, this individual was informing me that I did not indeed qualify as a financial sponsor. George informed me that the financial backers enjoy effortless income, whereas I did not possess any effortless income from my real estate venture. Consequently, I was perceived as lacking the attributes of a true investor.

Although it was not my preference to disclose it during that time, I must acknowledge that George was correct. I was required to renovate a residence and present it for remuneration. Provided that I ceased that particular course of action, I did not receive any form of recompense. There was no readily available source of income that would continue to sustain me in the event that I ceased working. Fundamentally, my primary occupation entailed the repair and subsequent sale of residential properties.

This was the juncture at which I grasped the differentiation between immediate transactions and enduring agreements. I consistently oversaw the temporary arrangements and never conceived of pursuing sustainable, revenue-generating ventures. Until then.

Subsequently, I initiated the acquisition of investment properties in order to augment our portfolio and cultivate a sustainable source of income. Over the course of a duration lasting approximately two to three years, Teresa and I were able to expand our portfolio by a total of 27 units, primarily comprising individual dwellings and a few modest multi-family properties.

Nevertheless, I made a concerted effort to steer clear of acquiring these newly sought-after investment properties. The aspiration of possessing an extensive portfolio decidedly surpassed the reality. I personally supervised all of them, and it seemed that there was a recurring matter to address. I believe that during that period, my passive income amounted to approximately $3000 per month.

However, it seemed that these tasks demanded a larger portion of my time in comparison to the typical recovery deal that I had initially anticipated earning $30,000 from.

I regrettably found these investment properties to be lacking in sustaining my interest.

In 2006, I was experiencing a sense of fatigue, and Teresa and I were presented with the opportunity to divest ourselves of exceptionally high-end hotel properties. I made the decision to present all of our investment properties to embark on this new endeavor.

We accumulated a substantial amount of capital when we liquidated our investment properties due to the appreciable increase in their value and market worth. I proudly exclaimed about our astuteness, as within a mere year of selling to them, the market experienced a severe downturn.

Nevertheless, the decision to sell those investment properties remains one of the gravest mistakes I have ever made in my real estate career. Furthermore, one of the most critical illustrations that I can provide at this present moment.

I have consistently been attracted to the fleeting real estate opportunities due to their predictable closure and often appealing financial rewards. I grappled with the protracted nature of my owned rental properties, as they appeared mundane and failed to ignite enthusiasm in me regarding their long-term prospects over a period spanning 15 to 20 years.

Utilizing Pivot Points in Options Day Trading

This strategy of day trading is especially advantageous in the realm of the Foreign Exchange Market. It delineates the practice of executing a pivot or reversal subsequent to the attainment of a support or resistance level at the prevailing market price. It functions in a manner identical to that of support and resistance breakouts.

The customary approaches associated with this specific form of options day trading are:

In the event that the support level is being approached, one may consider purchasing the position while subsequently setting a stop order slightly beneath the aforementioned level.

To initiate the sale of the position upon nearing the resistance level, subsequently establishing a stop order positioned slightly below that particular level.

In order to ascertain the pivot point, the day trader will conduct an analysis of the highest and lowest trading values of the prior day, as well as the closing prices from the same day. This is computed using the following equation:

The average of the high, low, and close prices equals the pivot point.

By employing the pivotal point, one can also derive the support and resistance levels. The equations representing the initial support and resistance levels are as follows:

The Second Pivot Point multiplied by two, subtracted from the High, results in the calculation of the First Support Level.

The initial level of resistance can be derived by subtracting the low point from twice the pivot point.

The second levels of support and resistance are derived using the subsequent mathematical equations:

The calculated value of the second support level can be determined by subtracting the pivot point from the difference between the first resistance level and the first support level.

The Second Resistance Level can be determined by calculating the Pivot Point, which is the difference between the First Resistance Level and the First Support Level.

The range of options trading that yields the highest profitability occurs when the pivot point falls within the range of the initial support and resistance levels.

The options day trader is exposed to abrupt price fluctuations due to his trading style. Failure to effectively manage this situation could lead to significant financial losses. In order to minimize potential losses using this approach, the options day trader can employ stop orders to mitigate and restrain the extent of any losses incurred. Typically, this is positioned slightly above the latest high price close when the day trader has initiated a short position. This is situated just beneath a recent low point, at which time the day trader had assumed a long position. In order to ensure an extra level of protection, the options day trader may also choose to employ two stop orders. These could involve setting a physical stop order at the maximum amount of capital that the trader is willing to risk, as well as implementing an exit strategy stop order for added security.

Generating Wealth through Real Estate Investment

Based on a statistical analysis, it has been determined that over 23% of the total residential property transactions in the year 2004 consisted of purchases made specifically for investment purposes. This is hardly

This is unexpected considering the substantial rise in property prices over the past years and the market's activity level.

significant returns.

There exists a multitude of avenues through which one may derive financial gains from the realm of real estate investments. When engaging in property flipping, one procures a property, promptly renovates it, and subsequently resells it for a lucrative gain.

An alternative means of acquiring investment property is by means of foreclosures, which transpire when a homeowner defaults on a loan, prompting the mortgage holder to conduct an auction for the property.

Due to the occasionally undisclosed ownership of abandoned properties, considerable efforts are devoted to conducting thorough title investigations and undertaking necessary legal procedures for such properties.

Investments in financial instruments, commonly referred to as intangible real estate assets.

Real estate-related investments materialize when individuals allocate funds into mutual funds or bonds that are directly linked to the performance of the real estate market, yet are distinct from physical properties themselves.

include physical property. These investments ought to be undertaken only after seeking guidance from a certified broker.

Control Your Exposure

It is imperative to effectively mitigate the risk associated with real estate investments.

protecting yourself from loss. Having a thorough understanding of the law is the utmost essential aspect of risk management in the real estate industry. It is imperative that you possess a comprehensive understanding of the legal framework and regulatory provisions pertaining to the field of real estate.

"After conducting an extensive investigation on the availability of properties, their respective pricing, and prospective buyers

In order to ascertain the interest, it is imperative to engage in informed speculation regarding the prospective developments in your market. Shall prices ascend or descend? Please be mindful of the following factors when evaluating the level of risk associated with your situation:

1. Consider the local economy. Is there employment opportunity currently accessible, or are the majority of businesses in the region undergoing workforce reduction? Is the rate of

residential development higher or lower compared to the previous five-year period?

2. Make sound financial decisions. When making a financial decision, it is important to take into consideration the duration for which you intend to retain ownership of the property.

source. Adjustable Rate Mortgages (ARMs) are regarded as enticing options owing to their diminished initial investments and comparatively lower interest rates.

You are granted the discretion to select the duration of the loan, typically ranging from one, two, or seven years. Upon the conclusion of this specified timeframe, the interest rate will be adjusted in line with prevailing rates. Should you desire to retain ownership of a property beyond the duration of an adjustable-rate mortgage (ARM), it is worth noting that the escalated interest rates associated with it will incur additional costs for you. It would be advisable to consider obtaining a fixed-rate mortgage with the most financially feasible term available to you.

Drawbacks associated with the 529 plan." "Demerits of the 529 plan." "Limitations of the 529 plan." "Detriments of the 529 plan." "Downsides of the 529 plan.

Similar to any savings account designed for long-term financial goals, we are strategically preparing for an optimal future. There exists the potentiality that you may encounter limitations in utilizing your 529 savings account for educational purposes due to a multitude of factors. Frequently, a family tends to save an excess amount for college and ends up with a surplus of funds in their 529 savings account. Should you indeed be resolute in your decision to refrain from utilizing these funds for personal or familial purposes, you will be liable to face a penalty of ten percent, in addition to meeting your obligation of fulfilling income tax liabilities to both state and federal authorities. I previously recommended that you allocate savings for only a portion equivalent to one fourth of your child's four-year education, and the justification for this advice is as follows. The consequences are severe, and it is advisable to err on the side of caution.

In the event that your child seeks federal student aid, it will be necessary to complete documentation pertaining to the household's financial circumstances. The primary determinant of student aid eligibility is dependency status.

However, if you designate your child as a dependent, the subsequent factor becomes whether or not you own a home. We will compile a comprehensive inventory of assets to ascertain the projected family contribution towards your child's expenses, in which the assets held within your 529 plan may be included. The classification of a 529 plan as an asset or not is contingent upon the regulations and policies established at the state level. It is highly probable that an increasing number of states will begin to designate 529 plans as a component of a family's asset portfolio, given the heightened imperative to ensure that federal funding is allocated to those individuals who are most in need. While it is not advisable to conceal your assets in order to pursue financial assistance for your child's education. It is important to highlight that your 529 account is anticipated to be included in a list of assessable assets by 2034.

There are two additional drawbacks that warrant discussion concerning the 529 plan. Although this problem is not frequently encountered, it is of significance to mention that the upper limit for contributions falls within the range of $300,000 to $500,000. The coverage of a 529 plan is contingent upon the regulations set forth by each respective state. However, if you possess a sizeable family and have intentions of financially supporting multiple children, it is probable that a 529 plan will not provide adequate funding for all. The 529 plan also curtails the range of investment opportunities available to you. This investment project is of a long-term nature and involves significant consequences for premature withdrawals. Withdrawing funds from your account, using them for more lucrative investments, and covering early withdrawal penalties may pose considerable challenges. It is advisable to presume that any funds contributed to a 529 account should not be contemplated for relocation until your child has reached the age of eighteen, at the very least.

The Cornerstone Metric

If I were to offer a singular crucial metric for your analysis and determination of whether to invest in that stock, it would unquestionably be the price-to-earnings ratio. It denotes the valuation ratio of the company, specifically measuring the relationship between the price and the earnings.

To acquire this numerical value, it is sufficient to perform the division of the stock's share price by its earnings-per-share. In order to achieve an impressive yield, it is necessary to attain a reduced P/E ratio. Due to a decreased ratio, there is a decrease in the amount of money required to purchase the stock, thereby substantiating the concept of value investing.

Nevertheless, exercise caution as the ratio may be diminished due to a deterioration in the company's operational efficiency or financial loss. Having a clear understanding of the optimal equilibrium is imperative.

There exist various approaches to ascertain the precise P/E ratio of the company, such as GAAP (Generally Accepted Accounting Principles) earnings and adjusted earnings, among others. GAAP represents the company's profit that remains unaffected by extraordinary occurrences, such as the receipt of tax incentives or acquisitions of business units.

These unforeseen non-sequential occurrences have the potential to induce a sudden and substantial increase or decrease in earnings. Hence, the modified formula yields a precise P/E ratio for investors to analyze closely. Each investor holds a divergent viewpoint on the P/E ratio. Individuals may perceive a specific ratio as promising, average, or unappealing, as their goals in terms of investments vary. Investors who engage in value investing tend to have a preference for stocks with a lower price-to-earnings (P/E) ratio. Additionally, one can derive other ratios analogous to the P/E metrics, such as the price/sales ratio or the price/book ratio, among others.

How To Sell Nfts?

NFTs are additionally retailed on various marketplaces, with the procedures differing from one platform to another. You will essentially upload your content onto a marketplace and then adhere to the instructions provided to transform it into an NFT. You will have the opportunity to incorporate details, such as a comprehensive description of the work and recommended pricing. The majority of Non-Fungible Tokens (NFTs) are acquired through the utilization of the Ethereum cryptocurrency, however, alternative ERC-20 tokens like WAX and Flow can also be utilized for purchase.

Can you please provide instructions on how to create a Non-Fungible Token (NFT)?

Any individual has the ability to generate an NFT. All that is required is a digital wallet, a modest acquisition of ethereum, and access to an NFT marketplace where you can upload and transform the content into an NFT or crypto art. Simple, right?

Non-fungible tokens, also known as NFTs, are experiencing a surge in popularity during the present period. Individuals are investing substantial sums of money in these exceptional collectible cryptocurrency assets. A single non-fungible token (NFT) created by the renowned digital artist Beeple was purchased for an astonishing sum of $69 million in the early months of 2021, whereas numerous other NFTs have commanded multimillion-dollar sales figures.

The promise of substantial financial gain is prompting an increasing number of individuals to generate NFTs with the aim of capitalizing on the current frenzy. "Presented below is a comprehensive sequential instructional manual elucidating the process of crafting (specifically minting) and commercializing a non-fungible token (NFT).

1. Choose your selection

Allow us to commence with the foundational elements. If you have not yet completed this task, it is necessary for you to ascertain which distinctive digital asset you intend to transform into a non-fungible token (NFT). It could manifest as a personalized artwork, image, musical composition, video game artifact, internet meme, animated graphic interchange format, or even a concise social media message. An NFT, or Non-Fungible Token, represents a distinct digital artifact that is exclusively owned by a single individual. The exceptional nature of the NFT bestows value upon it.

Ensuring that you possess the intellectual property rights for the item you intend to convert into an NFT is of utmost importance. Engaging in the creation of a non-fungible token (NFT) for a digital asset over which you lack legal ownership could potentially result in legal ramifications.

2. Please select your preferred blockchain

After choosing your distinctive digital asset, it is now time to initiate the process of minting it into a non-fungible token (NFT). The initial step involves identifying the blockchain technology you intend to leverage for your NFT. Ethereum (CRYPTO:ETH) holds utmost popularity among NFT artists and creators. Additional prominent choices encompass Tezos, Polkadot, Cosmos, and Binance Smart Chain.

3. Establish your digital wallet

If you do not already possess a digital wallet, it is advisable to establish one in order to facilitate the creation of your NFT, as you will require a certain amount of cryptocurrency to finance your initial investment. The wallet shall grant you access to your digital assets. The leading non-fungible token (NFT) wallets encompass notable platforms such as Metamask, Math Wallet, AlphaWallet, Trust Wallet, and Coinbase Wallet.

After establishing your digital wallet, it is advisable to acquire some cryptocurrency. The majority of NFT platforms readily embrace Ether, the cryptocurrency native to the Ethereum blockchain platform. If you presently possess any cryptocurrency from elsewhere, it would be advantageous to establish a connection between it and your digital wallet, enabling you to employ it for the purpose of generating and trading NFTs.

4. Choose your NFT marketplace.

After acquiring a digital wallet and a certain amount of cryptocurrency, it is now opportune to commence the process of generating (and, ideally, vending) your NFT. To accomplish this, it will be necessary for you to select an NFT marketplace. Some notable NFT marketplaces include OpenSea, Axie Marketplace, Larva Labs/CryptoPunks, NBA Top Shot Marketplace, Rarible, SuperRare, Foundation, Nifty Gateway, Mintable, and ThetaDrop.

You will be required to conduct thorough research on each NFT marketplace in order to identify a platform that aligns well with your NFT. As an illustration, one may consider the Axie Marketplace as the exclusive online retail platform catering to the highly renowned NFT game, Axie Infinity. In the meantime, NBA Top Shot operates as a marketplace with a primary focus on basketball. It is noteworthy to mention that certain marketplaces necessitate the use of their proprietary cryptocurrency. For instance, in the case of Rarible, the usage of Rarible (CRYPTO:RARI) is mandatory.

OpenSea generally serves as a favorable starting point. It provides the ability for individuals to create their own NFTs, thus establishing itself as a frontrunner in the realm of NFT transactions. In the month of August 2021, the NFT marketplace generated sales amounting to $3.4 billion through the purchase of NFTs.

Once you have chosen your preferred NFT marketplace, it will be necessary to establish a connection between it and your digital wallet. That will enable you to remit the requisite fees for minting your NFT and retaining any proceeds from sales.

5. Please proceed to upload your file.

You are now prepared to create your NFT. It is essential that the selected NFT marketplace provides a comprehensive, sequential tutorial to facilitate the process of uploading your digital file onto their platform. This procedure will facilitate the transformation of your digital file (such as a PNG, GIF, MP3, or any other file format) into a commercially viable NFT.

6. Establish the sales procedure

The ultimate phase in the process of NFT minting involves determining the preferred methodology for commercializing one's NFT. According to the particular platform, you have the ability to:

Establish a set price: By establishing a predetermined price, you enable the first interested individual willing to meet that specific price to purchase your NFT.

Establish a scheduled auction: A scheduled auction will afford potential NFT buyers a predetermined timeframe within which they can submit their ultimate bid.

Initiate an auction without restrictions: An unrestricted auction does not impose any time constraint. Conversely, you possess the authority to terminate the auction at your discretion.

You will be required to ascertain the minimum price (in the event of initiating an auction), establish the desired royalty rates to enable continued monetization of your NFT upon resale in the secondary market, and determine the optimal duration for conducting the auction (if timed). When determining the minimum price, it is essential to consider the associated fees, as setting a price that is too low may lead to financial loss in the sale of your NFT.

Regrettably, the expenses associated with the creation and commercialization of an NFT can be both substantial and intricate. Depending on the platform and pricing structure, you may be required to remit a listing fee, an NFT minting fee, a sales commission, and a transaction fee for transferring funds from the buyer's wallet to yours. Fluctuations in cryptocurrency pricing can also lead to variability in fees. Due to this factor, it is crucial to thoroughly examine the expenses associated with minting and selling your NFT to ensure their value justifies the investment.

Technical trading/charting

Technical chart analysis involves the examination of historical stock price charts in order to detect recurring patterns. These patterns frequently serve as indicators of future price movements.

The issue lies in the fact that these technical patterns at times prove to be completely unreliable indicators. While there are those who consider technical charting as a scientific approach, there are also critics who dismiss it as baseless conjecture.

An illustration of a technical charting terminology would be the occurrence of a 'double bottom' and 'double top'.

Technical trading refers to the practice of engaging in asset investment and trade decisions based on the analysis of charts.

Timing the market

This implies making purchases when prices have reached their minimum point. Makes sense, right? However, it must be acknowledged that accurately timing the market constitutes a formidable task, encompassing considerable challenges, despite the utilization of high-tech algorithms and vast resources available at prominent trading establishments. If you opt for a 'value investing' approach, market timing becomes unnecessary. This is due to the fact that a robust corporation, with sound fundamentals, will experience an appreciation in its worth irrespective of any unforeseen circumstances. The aforementioned holds true for stock markets as a whole. Rather than attempting to predict market fluctuations, one should opt to invest in a market index, such as the S&P 500 Index, and maintain a long-term investment strategy.

Value investing

Renowned investor Warren Buffet is widely recognized for his implementation of the 'value investing' approach. This implies identifying companies with robust underlying factors and attractive valuations, subsequently investing in them and retaining the stocks over an extended period of time.

Volatility

This terminology pertains to the degree of probability associated with the fluctuation of prices. Heightened volatility, as can be observed in the realm of cryptocurrency, results in swift and substantial fluctuations in prices. Low volatility, such as what is observed in the bond sector, signifies a state wherein price fluctuations occur at a languid and incremental pace.

Discovering Rental Properties: A Comprehensive Guide

Now that we have thoroughly examined the diverse advantages and risks associated with investing in real estate, as well as understanding the investor's mindset, it is essential for us to consider the approach we will adopt for our analysis.

When one is in search of a rental property, it is comprehensible that a plethora of alternatives are at one's disposal.

Nevertheless, you can employ the same approach while engaging in the process of property acquisition with the aim of subsequently generating rental income.

In the following chapter, we will explore various approaches to locating rental properties available for purchase.

Auctions

Auctions provide individuals with the opportunity to participate in the bidding process for a parcel of real estate. It would be advisable to maintain vigilance towards the diverse range of auctions that are available.

Internet-based auctions: Users will have the opportunity to browse and participate in property auctions through online platforms.

An auction of properties seized by the Sheriff is scheduled, encompassing various locations such as the county's hall of records, city hall, courtroom, and the sheriff's office. This is the primary location where the foreclosure sales will take place.

Exclusive auctions: These auctions typically involve a contractual arrangement between a lender and a multiple property sale, wherein numerous properties are presented for bidding simultaneously. These auctions are commonly conducted in a venue such as a conference center or, alternatively, potentially in a neighboring hotel establishment.

Advantage: more competitive pricing, access to properties not obtainable through conventional channels.

Drawback: The presence of competition may potentially prevent the acquisition of the desired property.

Foreclosed properties are frequently auctioned by the sheriff's office prior to being converted into real estate owned (REO) assets, which are subsequently listed and marketed by a local real estate agent.

Advantages: readily attainable

One drawback is that you are required to settle the remaining outstanding amount.

Driving by

These are properties that you will have the opportunity to visually assess as you engage in your routine daily tasks.

These can be effectively represented by an intermediary or alternatively, sold in a direct manner by the proprietor.

Advantage: Identify unspecified locations.

Disadvantage: There is a possibility of facing competition and potentially exceeding the original asking price.

Real estate agents or brokers can also aid you in the process of identifying properties that you may be interested in acquiring as an investment. They shall provide aid to facilitate the refinement of your search, taking into account specific criteria that you may seek. You also have the option of engaging the services of a professional agent to provide assistance.

- Reach out to the real estate agencies situated in specific localities to inquire about any prospective investment properties that may be currently on offer.

-Please feel free to contact us in regards to any properties you have observed while driving or that you may have come across on the internet.

- Possess the privilege of accessing the MLS database, which may not be readily available on websites.

Additionally, certain professional establishments may withhold from publishing property listings on the MLS, opting instead to exclusively share them with their trusted network of contacts.

In favor: The benefits of receiving personalized support and engaging in valuable professional connections.

Cons: It is necessary to remunerate an individual through a commission-based structure.

Networking

Engaging in networking can prove to be an excellent strategy for discovering rental properties that have yet to be publicized. Due to the property's limited public exposure, there is a greater likelihood of acquiring it at a price lower than the listed amount. When considering the aspect of networking, there exist multiple commendable groups which one can become a member of.

MUTUAL FUNDS

The utilization of shared assets is widely recognized as a viable approach for allocating resources towards safeguarding. Given that mutual funds provide inherent diversification and professional portfolio management, they confer distinct advantages compared to the purchase of individual equities and fixed-income securities. Nevertheless, like any investment in security, investing in a mutual fund entails distinct risks, including the potential for financial loss.

Recognized as an "open-end entity," a collective investment vehicle is an investment company that consolidates funds from multiple investors and allocates them according to predefined investment objectives. The company generates funding by issuing its own shares to investors. The funds are employed for the acquisition of a variety of stocks, bonds, short-term money market instruments, diverse securities or assets, or a combination of these investments. Every offer pertains to a proportional ownership stake in the asset, conferring to the investor a commensurate entitlement, based on their shareholding, to receive both income and capital gains derived from the asset's investments.

The investment decisions undertaken by an asset are determined by its objectives and, in the case of a well-managed fund, by the investment style and expertise of the asset's professional manager or managers. The assets held within the collective resource are referred to as its underlying investments, and the performance of those investments, net of asset costs, determine the investment return of the resource.

All the pertinent information regarding a collective asset, encompassing its investment approach, risk profile, historical performance, management, and fees, can be found in a document referred to as the summary. It is advisable to thoroughly review the outline before investing in an asset.

How They Work

Common assets hold intrinsic value, just like individual stocks. When you acquire shares of an asset, you assume partial ownership of said asset. This holds true for both security assets and stock assets, indicating a substantial distinction exists between owning an individual security and possessing an asset that lays claim to the bond. When an individual acquires a security, they are assured a predetermined rate of interest and the repayment of their principal amount. This is not the case with a security reserve, as it consists of a diverse range of securities with different interest rates and growth patterns. The value responsibility for reserve entitles individuals to a proportional share of the asset's accumulated interest, recognized capital gains, and the return in the event of its attachment to development.

If you possess stakes in a communal asset, you partake in its advantages. As an illustration, in cases where the undisclosed stocks or securities owned by the asset generate income in the form of dividends or interest, the asset distributes these earnings to its shareholders as payments called income allocations, minus any applicable expenses. In a similar vein, when the asset experiences gains from selling interests in its portfolio, it allocates those post-expense gains to investors as distributions of capital appreciation. You largely have the option of receiving these deliveries in cash or opting for their automatic reinvestment in order to augment the quantity of shares in your possession.

It is evident that charges must be paid on the asset's income distributions, as well as on its capital gains, if the asset is held in a taxable account. When you make an investment in a mutual fund, you may incur short-term capital gains, which are subject to the same tax rate as your regular income - a scenario you may seek to avoid when liquidating your individual securities. In the event that the asset sells certain holdings for a higher price than their initial acquisition cost, you may also be liable for capital gains taxes, irrespective of whether the asset's overall profitability is negative for the year. This holds true even if you became an investor in the asset after it acquired those aforementioned holdings.

Regardless, if you possess the shared asset in a qualifying or tax-exempt account, such as an individual retirement account, no tax liability arises upon the receipt of these distributions. Regardless, you will be responsible for a fee at your standard rate for any withdrawals made from a duty deferred account.

You can also generate income from your holdings in the asset by either selling them back to the asset or redeeming them, provided that the underlying interests in the asset have appreciated in value since the time of your initial share purchase. Taking everything into account, your advantage will be the increase in the per-share value of the asset, also known as its net asset value or NAV. In a similar vein, charges are anticipated in the fiscal year when one realizes profits from an accessible account, yet not in a conceded or tax-exempt account. The determination of capital additions for shared assets differs somewhat from gains for individual investments, and annually, the asset will allocate your portion of the asset's profits.

Comparing Open-End and Closed-End Investment Funds

A notable characteristic of a mutual fund, or open-ended investment vehicle, is the ability for investors to buy or sell shares at their discretion. The reserves are presenting fresh proposals to address the demand for increased transactions and to accommodate the sale of shares by investors. Occasionally, open-end reserves become so substantial that they are closed to fresh investors. Irrespective of the closure of an open-end fund, it continues to maintain its open-end nature as existing shareholders retain their ability to engage in the trading of fund shares.

Open-end reserves determine the value of a single investment, referred to as the net asset value (NAV), once daily upon the closure of the investment market. All purchases and transactions made throughout the day are documented at the Net Asset Value mentioned. In order to compute the net asset value (NAV) of an asset, it is necessary to consider the total value of its investment assets, subtract the asset's expenses and costs, and then divide this amount by the number of shares held by investors.

The net asset value (NAV) of an asset does not truly represent its prosperity in the same way as stock prices do. Due to the perpetual nature of open-end assets, they undergo a continuous cycle of issuing fresh offers and repurchasing existing ones, resulting in a constant flux of both the quantity of offers and the monetary investment in the asset. Therefore, it is advisable to examine the overall return over time when comparing two supports, rather than solely considering their NAVs.

Closed-end reserves differ from open-end reserves in that they raise funds only once through a single contribution, similar to how a stock issue raises funds for the company only once, during its initial public offering, or IPO. Upon the completion of the sale of the offers, the closed-end store proceeds to leverage the capital to acquire a diverse range of underlying investments. Consequently, any subsequent growth of the fund hinges solely upon the returns generated by its investments, rather than new investment funds. The asset is subsequently registered in a transaction similar to that of a individual stock, allowing for continuous trading throughout the day.

You can engage in the trading of shares of a closed-end store by submitting the request to your designated stockbroker. The expenses associated with closed-end subsidies fluctuate based on investor demand and may exceed or fall below their net asset value (NAV), which represents the actual per-share value of the fund's underlying investments.

How to Engage in Cryptocurrency Investment

Investing in cryptocurrencies can present an intriguing opportunity to explore the realms of both commerce and technology. One of the fundamental principles that we have consistently emphasized throughout the course of this book is to invariably allocate your investments in instruments that you possess a comprehensive comprehension of. Therefore, it is advisable for individuals who do not possess advanced skills in cryptocurrencies to acquire substantial knowledge regarding these digital assets prior to making any investment decisions. Hence, this publication serves as an excellent point of embarkation.

Generally speaking, investing in cryptocurrencies can be likened to investing in any other type of financial instrument available. Nonetheless, it is imperative that you thoroughly consider the rationale behind your contemplation of venturing into cryptocurrencies. Therefore, it is imperative to commence the process by determining the underlying motive for investing in this particular asset class.

In a broader sense, there exist two primary rationales for engaging in cryptocurrency investments: the pursuit of either short-term profitability or long-term returns.

If your primary objective entails pursuing immediate profits, cryptocurrencies may not align with your objectives. You may observe that the cryptocurrency market is not as fully matured as the foreign exchange (FOREX) market. Under such circumstances, the foreign exchange market (FOREX) excels in generating profits in the short-term.

What's the reason?

The considerable magnitude of the trading volume in the foreign exchange market is substantial. This market operates continuously, round the clock, with no interruptions. Consequently, a lack of action is not apparent. The stock market ceases operations daily and remains closed during weekends. Therefore, it proves to be challenging to engage in trading with the intention of achieving short-term profitability.

With regard to this matter, the term "short-term" pertains to the act of maintaining positions for a duration of mere minutes.

That is an action that is presently unavailable with cryptocurrencies, or at the very least, has not been developed thus far. In a broader context, it can be observed that cryptocurrency investors commonly maintain their holdings for a range of days. Consequently, it is advisable not to anticipate significant market activity unless there were abrupt occurrences with substantial market impacts. Therefore, if your primary objective is to achieve immediate profits, cryptocurrency may not be the most suitable option.

Hence, cryptocurrencies are more suitable for long-term investment endeavors. With regards to this matter, our intention is to define "long-term" as a duration extending for more than a month. Indeed, a majority of cryptocurrency holders demonstrate a propensity to engage in short-term trading, typically liquidating their holdings within a span of approximately 30 days. This is attributed to the insufficient trading activity observed in other markets.

Moreover, due to the limited trading volume of cryptocurrencies, changes in price movement often occur at a relatively slower pace compared to what one would typically anticipate. Therefore, it is advisable to bear this in consideration. However, if you are prepared to maintain your current positions for an extended period, there is potential for generating satisfactory returns.

The inquiry at present arises as to how one may commence their investment endeavors in cryptocurrencies.

There exist several methodologies.

One option is to proactively address the situation. Due to the relatively limited regulatory oversight compared to other types of assets, one can engage in the buying and selling of cryptocurrencies with a similar transactional approach to selling a vehicle. However, when considering the purchase and sale of cryptocurrencies, gold serves as the most suitable analogy.

Investment-grade gold bullion is available for purchase from any authorized dealer. Your sole responsibility lies in ensuring that they do not engage in fraudulent activities by selling counterfeit gold. Subsequently, you have the option to physically acquire the gold, or alternatively, proceed to your designated merchant and personally retrieve it. Afterwards, you have the option to safely store the gold within the confines of your residence. Alternative gold investors opt for the payment of third-party storage services. This indicates that they will engage the services of a professional vault company to securely store their gold, instead of maintaining it within their residence. This option is significantly more secure, especially in the case where they possess a considerable quantity of gold.

This analogy proves incredibly efficacious in the realm of cryptocurrencies, as it exemplifies the direct acquisition of cryptos sans the intermediation of brokers or investment companies. Subsequently, you have the option to store them within your electronic wallet. This solution presents a significantly more pragmatic approach compared to the alternative of engaging the services of a vault company. To put it in a figurative sense, you are indeed in possession of it, although it does not exist as a tangible vault.

When engaging in the acquisition of cryptocurrencies directly from individual holders, one can accomplish this transaction by utilizing a digital currency exchange platform like Coinbase. In this transaction, a multitude of individuals convene with the objective of engaging in the purchase and sale of cryptocurrencies. The assurance provided in this transaction is that users undergo a verification process. Rest assured, you are ensured by the exchange that no fraudulent activities will occur. This aspect should be given due consideration, especially if you are contemplating the direct acquisition of cryptocurrencies from another individual. It is advisable to refrain from engaging in transactions of this nature unless you possess knowledge of the parties involved and have established a high level of trust with them.

After acquiring your initial crypto holding, you may proceed to patiently anticipate an increase in price. Subsequently, you have the opportunity to engage in profitable resale. It's really that straightforward. Nevertheless, the caveat lies in patiently anticipating the point at which the price ascends sufficiently to yield a profitable return. Henceforth, it is imperative to retain the awareness that prices undergo fluctuations. It is imperative for you to thoroughly research and gather information on this matter. Platforms such as Coinbase closely monitor the price fluctuations of every cryptocurrency available for trading on their platform. This tool proves invaluable as it enables the analysis of price action trends. This will assist you in determining whether it is advantageous to engage in the activity or rather abstain until a more advantageous opportunity presents itself.

Additionally, there are exchange-traded funds (ETFs) specializing in cryptocurrencies.

This investment instrument is relatively recent in nature as cryptocurrencies have not been in existence for an extensive period of time. From this perspective, brokers possess limited proficiency in trading cryptocurrencies. Although the returns of crypto ETFs may not demonstrate the same level of stability commonly exhibited by other conventional ETFs, investing in a crypto ETF could prove beneficial for individuals seeking to gain exposure to this market while maintaining a preference for non-active trading.

It is important to highlight that cryptocurrency ETFs are extensively available. Therefore, it may be necessary for you to conduct a thorough search in order to locate a broker with the requisite expertise to engage in trading in this particular field. There is, however, a caveat to consider: given the comparatively relaxed regulations surrounding cryptocurrencies, your assurances mostly depend on the reputation of the broker rather than any other concrete guarantees. It is imperative to ensure that you are engaging with individuals of high repute. By doing so, you can ensure that you do not fall victim to fraudulent activities orchestrated by anonymous cryptocurrency investors.

Useful Resources

To excel in value investing, one must possess pertinent information. It is imperative that you possess an understanding of the specific information you ought to seek initially, as well as the appropriate sources through which to obtain it. This is the subject matter that will be addressed in this chapter, prior to delving into the diverse range of techniques available for implementing value investing strategies.

Key Considerations for a Value Investor

As a practitioner of value investing, you embody the characteristics of both a scientist and an artist. This implies that you seek out information that cannot be readily quantified, as well as information that is inherently immeasurable. Measurable actions pertain to numerical data and equations that facilitate the assessment of a business's worth. The immeasurable component involves leveraging your expertise and discernment to ascertain the potential outcomes that could arise from the decision to acquire a company. This is the modus operandi of the market, thanks to the diverse methodologies employed for its interpretation and the assortment of viewpoints held in regard to it.

It is important to note that an excess of information can result in significant confusion. Therefore, it is advisable to extract the necessary information from a minimum of two to three reliable sources, diligently acquire knowledge from each source, and frequent their utilization.

Essential Information for Your Acquaintance

Financial results matter. You should obtain access to the financial statements of the company you are involved with, in order to ascertain its liabilities, assets, growth, and earnings. You will obtain an overview of all these elements, including the net worth, by referring to the balance sheet. In regard to the expenditures, revenues, and profits during a specified timeframe, you may acquire this information from the income statement. Of equal significance is the cash flow statement, which outlines the sources of the company's cash inflows and delineates the allocation of cash resources.

Financial trends matter, too. Merely examining the latest financial statements is insufficient; one must also consider the company's historical data. Trends exhibit a recurring pattern that is prone to replication. As customary, historical performance should not serve as a reliable indicator of future outcomes; nevertheless, the utilization of past data can prove instrumental in discerning prospective developments. The fact that there has been sustained growth for a consecutive period of four years is quite commendable. However, an extended period of growth spanning a decade would be deemed even more favorable. It is imperative to consistently monitor the prevailing trend within your organization.

It is imperative to conduct a comprehensive analysis of your company vis-à-vis other entities operating within the same industry. This pertains to establishing ratios that enable you to assess the relative profitability, efficiency, financial stability, and quality of your company, all of which contribute to its overall value. It is advisable to refrain from utilizing percentages, such as return on assets (ROA), return on equity (ROE), net and gross profit margin.

Conducting a thorough analysis of market data is an excellent means of gauging the prospective outcomes for the company in the times ahead. Therefore, it is imperative that you comprehend the customer demographic, market penetration, and growth in sales volume, as these parameters hold significant importance. Companies typically refrain from disclosing this information as a means to maintain a competitive edge. Therefore, it is necessary to rely on the information provided by the company itself or seek independent analysis from third-party sources.

To clarify, it is important to note that market information is entirely independent of trends, past stock price movements, or technical analysis pertaining to stock prices. What it entails is essentially the corporation's performance within its designated market, where it vends its products and services. That\\\'s it.

Operating facts are also of equal usefulness. These tools afford you the opportunity to conduct comparative assessments of your company vis-à-vis others, or can serve to fortify your examination of the financial state of the company. Indicators such as the extent of operations, quantity of outlets and workforce, among other factors, can provide insights into the efficiency and productivity of the company.

Art

Art holds no correlation with the securities market, thus implying that artworks can appreciate in value even during periods of market downturn. However, it is important to note that art is a highly illiquid asset.

Artwork may necessitate a considerable duration for successful auctioning; therefore, if one intends to invest, it is advisable to regard art investing as a medium to long-term augmentation to their portfolio. Engaging in the field of art can pose inherent risks. Artisans and their craftsmanship permeate across aesthetics, exerting influence on the monetary value in terms of resale and return on investment.

The procurement of art entails significant supplementary costs, such as fees for commissions and measures for preservation. The primary peril lies in the ever-present possibility of counterfeit activities, theft, or harm.

Engaging the services of a skilled construction consultant is highly recommended, while also ensuring a clear distinction between your preferences and dislikes.

Gaining knowledge and expanding your education presents the paramount and unmistakable chance requisite for achieving any form of accomplishment.

Authentic artifacts are highly valued, although even a replica can possess some intrinsic worth.

Craftsmanship as an investment may not be suitable for all individuals. It often proves to be quite fulfilling, however, there is no guarantee that the artwork you purchase will appreciate in value.

Benefits derived from investing in the field of art:

• Physical asset

• Enjoyment value

• It has the potential to appreciate in value over time.

• Refrain from displaying variations in order to prevent exposure

• Expand the variety within your investment portfolio

"The hindrance of allocating investments towards artistic endeavors.

• Insufficient information poses a barrier to entry. • The absence of adequate information serves as an obstacle to entry. • Inadequate access to information constitutes a hurdle to entry.

• This asset lacks liquidity • Inadequate liquidity of the asset • Insufficient liquidation potential of the asset

• The task of taking care can prove to be challenging.

• There is no guarantee of appreciation in value over the course of time.

• Forgeries

• Insurance costs

• Storage

• You may become a target for thieves. • You are susceptible to being targeted by thieves. • Thieves may view you as a potential target. • You could potentially be the object of interest for thieves. • You are at risk of being singled out by thieves.

One can acquire artistic creations through the means of bartering, attending exhibitions, participating in art fairs, and accessing them online.

Jewellery

Jewelry can be regarded as an ardent investment, and as such, it holds significant value. In the scenario where you obtain them from renowned designers across the globe, these items will retain their value.

Distinguished planners are renowned for incorporating exquisite gemstones and precious metals in each design, significantly enhancing their intrinsic worth.

The price of diamonds can fluctuate significantly, driven by factors such as color, consumer preferences, and market demand, thus exhibiting resilience against inflation.

In contrast to gold, precious gemstones do not possess a standardized price per carat. The value of each gemstone is determined by a combination of carat, color, clarity, and cut.

Gold generally represents a secure investment; however, on the other hand, diamonds frequently possess a higher resale value, rendering them more valuable. Apart from precious gems, there has been a substantial surge in the demand for gemstones.

Platinum, due to its extraordinary and scarce attributes, consistently carries a higher price tag than gold; however, it is important to note that diamonds surpass all in terms of expense.

Jewelry originating from particular contemporary epochs tends to command higher prices. The artistry of Art Deco jewelry from the 1920s and 1930s is currently experiencing a resurgence.

Certain precious stones and renowned brands have maintained their intrinsic value over the course of time. Names such as

Cartier and Van Cleef and Arpels serve as exemplary illustrations of conspicuous excellence.

"Benefits of investing in jewellery:

• They are highly noticeable advantages

• They are impervious to hacking or deletion.

• They can be easily transported

Drawbacks of allocating resources towards the acquisition of jewellery:

• Cost

- Storage

- They do not possess liquidity as investments

- They do not provide remuneration or any form of compensation.

They can be acquired from reputable retailers or via auction platforms.

Wine

Exquisite wine undergoes transformation after bottling and progressively enhances its quality as it matures. Across the globe, there is a growing demand and increasing value associated with exquisite wine.

The various classifications of wine include white, red, rosé, dessert or sweet, and sparkling varieties.

You may engage the services of a reputable vendor to leverage their expertise in facilitating the acquisition of high-quality investment-grade wine. It is strongly recommended that you seek guidance when investing in wine as not all widely known wines are suitable for investment purposes.

You are allocating resources to a limited-production resource that has a significant global demand.

Given the lack of regulations in this market, it is advisable to procure goods exclusively from established and reputable suppliers to ensure the required level of aptitude.

Short-term gains have been conceivable, however, it is important to consider a mid to long-term perspective when making your investment. A period of approximately five years should be considered as the norm, while a range of eight to ten years would be even more desirable.

Typically, it is predominantly the wines that are explicitly stated or specified that tend to accrue value, and such wines generally come with a higher price tag. Do not engage in transactions with any wine speculation firms that approach you through unsolicited communication.

Contribute solely on the basis of your confident expertise in managing fine wine, or on the assurance that you have a trusted acquaintance well-versed in this domain.

Do not purchase wines that are older than 15 years unless you possess sufficient knowledge in the matter, given that the risk of counterfeit wine increases significantly with vintage age.

Ensure that the bottles of wine are properly placed within their distinct wooden enclosure and form a complete ensemble.

Benefits of allocating investments to the wine industry:

• Provides enticing investment opportunities

• Less volatile

• Global demand

Drawbacks of allocating resources towards the wine industry:

• Insufficient market liquidity • Inadequate liquidity levels • Deficiency in the availability of liquid assets • Scarcity of market liquidity • Limited access to liquid funds

• The substantial cost associated with storage • The considerable expenditure required for storage • The significant financial burden of storing

• Elevated commission selling charge

• Fake wines

• Unregulated market

One can acquire premium quality wine by attending in-person auctions, participating in online auctions, utilizing online wine trading platforms, visiting specialty stores, or purchasing directly from vineyards.